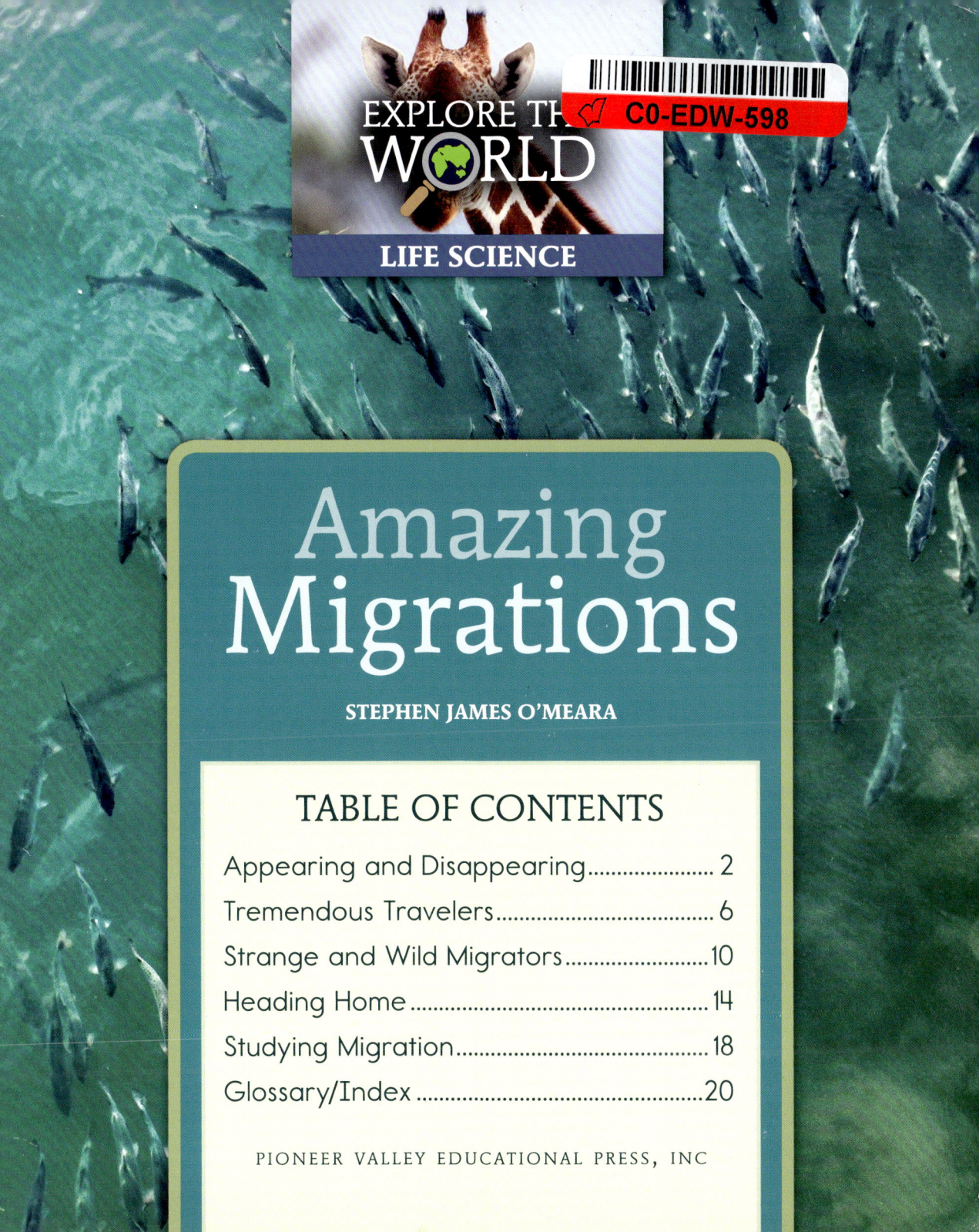

EXPLORE THE WORLD
LIFE SCIENCE

Amazing Migrations

STEPHEN JAMES O'MEARA

TABLE OF CONTENTS

Appearing and Disappearing 2
Tremendous Travelers 6
Strange and Wild Migrators 10
Heading Home 14
Studying Migration 18
Glossary/Index 20

PIONEER VALLEY EDUCATIONAL PRESS, INC

APPEARING AND DISAPPEARING

From whales to butterflies, animals around the globe are on the move. Have you noticed geese flying south for the winter or the seasonal appearance of seals off the coast? You've probably seen the almost clockwork-like appearance and disappearance of certain bird species in the spring and fall.

While most of us anticipate the comings and goings of animals that visit our neighborhoods, some scientists are gaining a more **global** understanding of migrations, these seasonal mass movements of animals. Millions of creatures undertake these extraordinary journeys of survival each year. Here are some of the most mysterious—and perhaps most unknown—fascinating migrations.

MORE TO EXPLORE

During its nine-day journey, the **BAR-TAILED GODWIT** can fly for more than 7,000 miles without stopping for rest or food. That's the longest-ever recorded nonstop flight for a bird.

3

In late summer and early fall, great white sharks appear along the US coast of the North Pacific in an area called the Red (Blood) Triangle. They arrive at the Farallon Islands, off the coast of San Francisco, where they feed on newborn seal pups.

By December, the sharks head back out to deeper waters. Great white sharks are known to gather in a remote spot in the Pacific Ocean, halfway between Hawaii and Baja California, though researchers are still trying to figure out why they go there.

How do they manage to travel so far in open sea where food is scarce? Researchers believe one of the ways may be that sharks store reserves of fat they get from eating seal and whale blubber in waters along the coast. Blubber is rich in fat and provides the sharks with the energy to make the long trip.

Great white sharks get their name from their white underbelly.

TREMENDOUS TRAVELERS

Arctic terns are the undisputed migration **marathon** champs. Each year, they fly from the Arctic to the Antarctic—a round trip of around 44,000 miles. They leave the Arctic in the fall. Most fly over the Atlantic Ocean, following the west coast of Africa until they reach Antarctica. Others initially follow a similar Atlantic journey but then make their way past Brazil on their way to Antarctica.

In its lifetime, it is estimated that an Arctic tern flies the equivalent of three trips to the moon and back.

In late spring, they snake their way northward, flying in a large-scale S-shaped path up the center of the Atlantic Ocean. Because the terns are in both the Arctic and Antarctic during each region's longest days of the year, they see more daylight than any other living creature!

Many insects migrate together in large groups. Their journeys help them find better food, a safer place to lay their eggs, or a warmer or cooler climate as the seasons change.

Some migrate just one way. When they get to their new location, they breed. The next generation then migrates back to the starting location. Other insects migrate from a breeding area to a feeding zone, where food is more plentiful. A third group migrates from a breeding location to a hibernation site.

MORE TO EXPLORE

Millions of monarch butterflies migrate from southern Canada to California or Mexico, where they **SPEND THE WINTER** in the warmer climate. In late winter or early spring, the adults travel north and lay eggs.

Desert locusts usually live alone. But these creatures can be incredibly damaging because they occasionally join together in huge swarms. This transformation results from hunger. During a drought, **solitary** locusts are forced closer together as they eat from the same small patches of plants. The locusts migrate great distances together to find new food sources. Forty to 80 million ravenous locusts may travel together, devouring crops and vegetation as they move.

A locust can eat its own weight in plants each day.

STRANGE AND WILD MIGRATORS

The red crabs of Christmas Island in the Indian Ocean journey on one of the most bizarre migrations known. At the beginning of the wet season, about 50 million of these land crabs scurry from the forest to the coast, where they breed, then lay eggs in the sea.

>> **Red crabs dig their own burrows throughout the rain forest. For much of the year, they live there alone.**

The two-to-three-week journey involves climbing down high cliff faces, marching through human settlements, and crossing highways. If the crabs are caught in unshaded heat, they die; about half a million are killed crossing streets. The crabs travel quickly to prevent **dehydration** in the hot sun. Their migration is linked to the phases of the moon so that eggs may be released into the sea precisely at the turn of the high tide.

MORE TO EXPLORE

Red crabs stop traffic, **PUNCTURE TIRES**, and wander through open doors as they migrate from the forest to the sea.

Every year, around the end of the wet season in the spring, Africa's Serengeti Plain is the site of the greatest wildlife show on Earth. Some 200,000 zebras, 500,000 gazelles, and 1.2 million wildebeests follow the rains and cross some of the continent's most spectacular landscapes.

The main migration starts in Tanzania, where the animals **calve** between January and mid-March. The group then heads north into the Serengeti's western corridor, almost as far as Lake Victoria. When the grass supply has been exhausted, usually at the end of summer, the herds move farther north to the Kenyan border before returning to their breeding grounds. By the time they arrive, the grounds are green and lush once more.

By the end, the animals will have covered many miles—provided that they successfully avoid the multitude of lions, leopards, cheetahs, crocodiles, and hyenas who must see the great migration as a giant feast!

MORE TO EXPLORE

Beginning each July, **A POPULAR SAFARI ATTRACTION** involves watching animals cross the Grumeti and Mara Rivers as crocodiles lie waiting.

13

HEADING HOME

Green sea turtles leave their feeding grounds off the coast of Brazil to begin a remarkable 2,500-mile round-trip journey to a tiny, remote island in the South Atlantic Ocean. Adult turtles make this trip every three to four years. The turtles swim for five to six weeks through open ocean to nest, it appears, on the very beaches where they were born.

Green sea turtles weigh up to 600 pounds and are among the largest sea turtles in the world.

After their young are born, the turtles return to the coast of Brazil. Scientists are not sure how the turtles find the tiny island in a vast ocean, so the journey is an amazing **navigational** feat.

MORE TO EXPLORE

Green sea turtles are listed as an **ENDANGERED SPECIES,** but they are still killed for their meat and eggs.

Loggerhead turtles migrate in enormous circles in both the Atlantic and Pacific Oceans. The Pacific route takes them from Japan to Mexico and back again. That's a 15,000-mile round trip, one of the longest migrations recorded for any turtle.

>> **Loggerhead turtles can live more than 50 years in the wild.**

16

A third of Japan's loggerhead turtles nest on Yakushima Island. One of them, which spent a year at the Okinawa Churaumi Aquarium before being tagged and released in 1988, was recaptured six years later... in Mexico!

STUDYING MIGRATION

How do we know so much about animals and their migrations? Scientists were studying animal, bird, and insect migrations in 1899 when a Danish teacher visited starling nests and placed an aluminum leg band on each bird **engraved** with a number and an address. Anyone who found the bird could send information about the time and place it was found.

a flock of starlings

This is called birdbanding. We now have tracking devices that use radio or satellite transmitters to follow the incredible, breathtaking migrations of animals around the world.

MORE TO EXPLORE

The North American Bird Banding Program, which includes research in the United States and Canada, manages **MORE THAN 77 MILLION** archived banding records that date back to the 1920s.

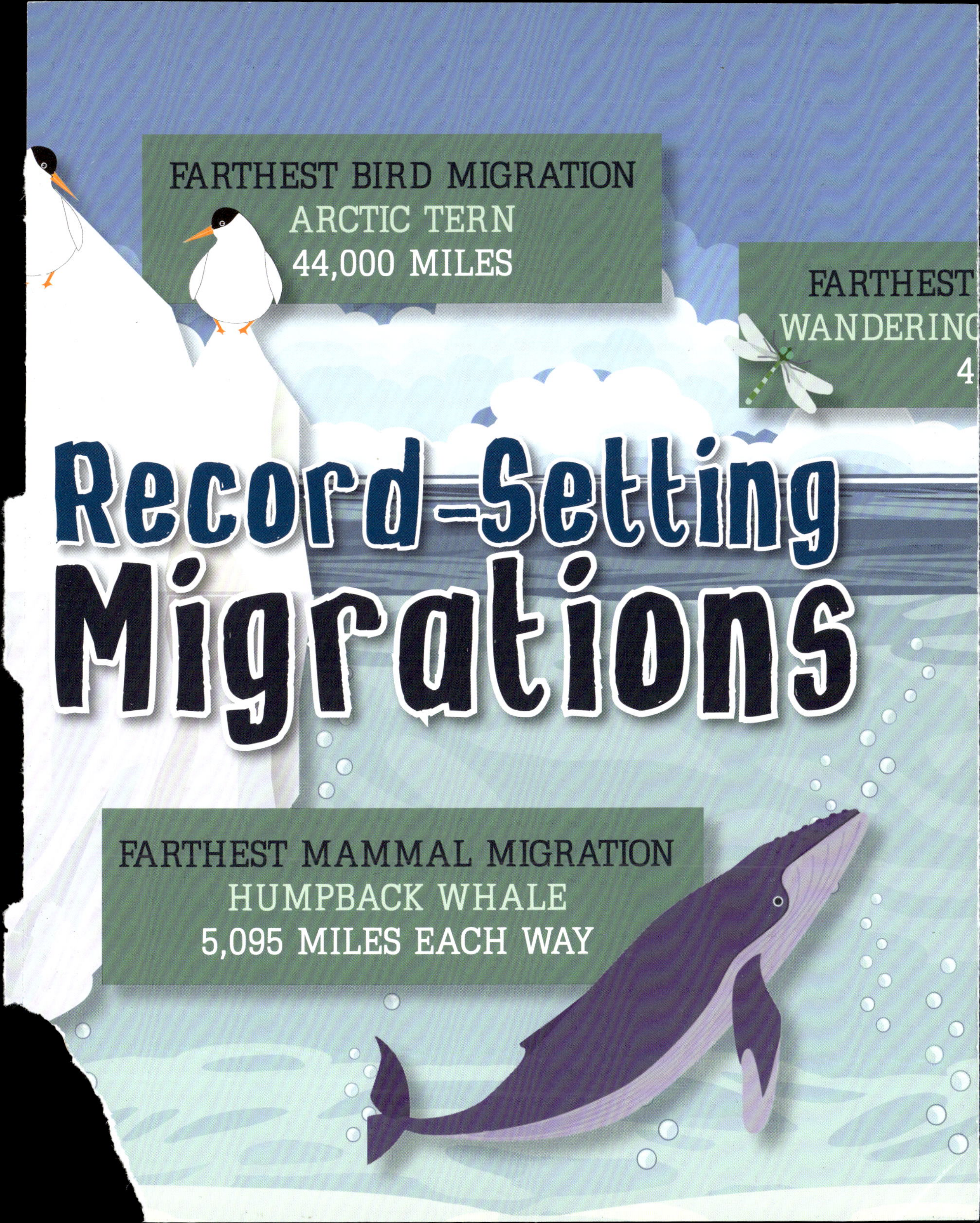

FARTHEST BIRD MIGRATION
ARCTIC TERN
44,000 MILES

FARTHEST WANDERING
4

Record-Setting Migrations

FARTHEST MAMMAL MIGRATION
HUMPBACK WHALE
5,095 MILES EACH WAY

GLOSSARY

calve
to give birth

dehydration
the state of losing too much water

engraved
formed by carving something onto or into a hard surface

global
involving the whole world

marathon
something that involves a long distance or takes a lot of time or a great deal of work

navigational
involving the act of moving from place to place

solitary
alone

INDEX

Africa 6, 12
Antarctic 6–7
Arctic 6–7
Arctic terns 6–7
Atlantic Ocean 6–7, 14, 16
bar-tailed godwit 3
birdbanding 19
calve 12
crocodiles 13
dehydration 11
endangered species 15
engraved 18
gazelles 12
geese 2
global 3
great white sharks 4–5
green sea turtles 14–15
Indian Ocean 10
insect 8, 18
locusts 9
loggerhead turtles 16–17
marathon 6
monarch butterflies 8
navigational 15
North American Bird Banding Program 19
red crabs 10–11
seals 2, 4, 5
Serengeti Plain 12
solitary 9
starlings 18
wildebeests 12
zebras 12

20